GOLD

Sarah Fleming

Introduction	2
Shiny	4
Soft	6
Bendy	8
Gold lasts forever	9
Gold conducts electricity	10
Gold conducts and reflects heat	11
Gold is money	12
Gold is rare	14
Finding Gold	15
Mali	15
Ghana	16
USA	18
South Africa	19
Panning for gold	20
5 Facts about Gold	21
The Midas touch	22
Look back and Index	23
Glossary	24

Introduction

The word 'gold' comes from an Anglo-Saxon word for yellow – 'gelo'.

Other languages have words for gold that sound nearly the same: **Gold** (German), **Guld** (Danish), **Gulden** (Dutch), **Gull** (Norwegian) and **Kulta** (Finnish).

Gold is used for lots of things. It has many useful properties. It:
- is shiny.
- is soft.
- is bendy.
- lasts forever.
- conducts electricity.
- conducts and reflects heat.

There is not much gold in the world. People want it because it is rare and this also makes it expensive.

Shiny

Gold is shiny. It is a warm colour like the sun. People have always worn gold as jewellery because it is shiny.

The Ancient Egyptians thought the sun was a god. They thought their king, the pharaoh, was a god too. The king wore gold to look like the sun.

Pharaoh Tutankhamun was buried with:
- 500 gold statues.
- gold beds and chairs.
- jewellery made of solid gold, gold leaf and gold wire.
- gold sandals.
- gold caps on his toes.

He was buried in:
- two wooden outer coffins, covered in gold.
- an inner coffin made of solid gold, weighing 110.4 kg.

He was buried wearing:
- a gold mask. It weighed 11 kg and was 2 cm thick.
- a 30 cm long solid gold dagger.

In South America, the Incas thought that the sun was god, and that gold was the 'sweat of the sun'. They made many objects out of gold, including death masks.

Jewellery is only the third most important use of gold today. Can you guess what else gold is used for? Read on!

SOLID GOLD FACT

In 1380 AD the King of Spain made a new law: No one could wear gold except his queen and princesses.

Soft

Gold can be flattened if you hit it with a hammer.

Gold can be hammered into sheets.

Very, very thin gold sheets can be put onto other things to make them look like gold. This kind of gold is called gold leaf.

SOLID GOLD FACT
You can make a sheet of gold so thin you can see through it!

To make it stronger, gold is often mixed with other metals, like silver. You can find out how much gold is in something by finding out what carat it is. Pure gold is 24 carat.

Definition
carat, (say 'CARR-ot'): This is a measure of the amount of pure gold in an object. The higher the carat the purer the gold. Most jewellery is made of 9 or 18 carat gold. This gold is harder and will not bend easily.

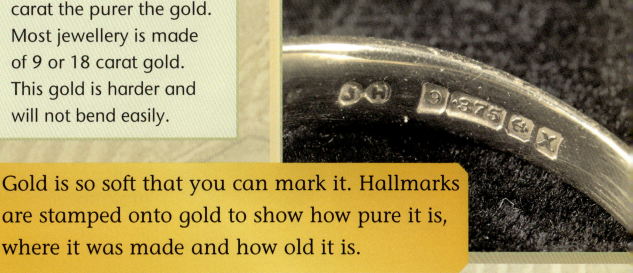

Gold is so soft that you can mark it. Hallmarks are stamped onto gold to show how pure it is, where it was made and how old it is.

You would put this set of hallmarks on something to say:

  The gold was checked in Sheffield.

  The gold is 18 carat gold.

  The item was made in Sheffield.

  The item is made of gold.

  The item was made in 2003.

Bendy

This is a necklace called a 'torc'. It was made in Iron Age Britain, about 75BC. 64 threads of gold and silver have been twisted around each other, to make eight ropes, which are twisted and made into a torc. The ends are hollow gold. The necklace weighs over 1 kg – that's like carrying one bag of sugar round your neck!

Gold can be pulled into wires. This is good for making jewellery.

In about 25AD Boudica, the Iceni Queen who fought with the Romans, was said to have worn a gold necklace that probably looked just like this.

What else could thin gold wires be used for?

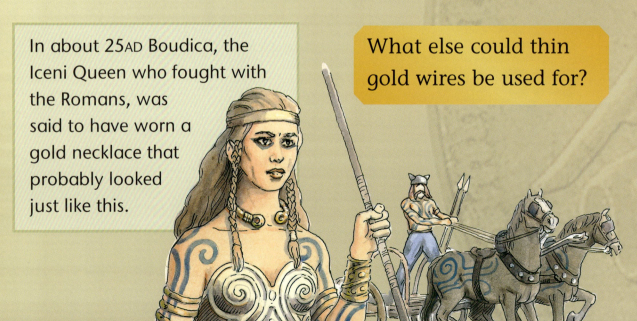

Gold lasts forever

old gold

old iron

Gold does not rust.

Gold lasts forever. It is used to make fillings for teeth, and for making false teeth. This is the second most important use of gold today.

SOLID GOLD FACT

These gold teeth were made for a Roman about 2000 years ago. They are still good enough to use today!

Gold conducts electricity

Gold is a conductor of electricity. It can also be stretched and it does not rust. These properties make gold very important in machines run by electricity.

 A normal phone has 33 gold parts.

Gold is expensive, so it is often put on wires as a thin outside layer.

There is gold inside every computer. There is gold inside most calculators and televisions. More gold is used in machines than in anything else today.

Gold conducts and reflects heat

Gold is a good conductor of heat. If you heat up a small bit of something that is gold, the heat will spread quickly and evenly through all of it.

Gold reflects heat. There is a thin layer of gold in the walls of space shuttles. This helps to keep heat away from the astronauts and the equipment inside.

Gold is even used in the glass of these windows. A very thin layer of it keeps the heat out in the summer, and in the winter it keeps the heat in.

A thin film of gold on this suit and mask helps to protect the fire fighter in very hot fires.

Gold is money

Gold has been used to trade with for thousands of years.

In China, gold squares were used as money 3000 years ago.

King Croesus (say 'Cree-sus') invented gold coins in about 550 BC.
- He was rich (have you heard of the phrase 'As rich as Croesus'?).
- He once gave a priest 117 bars of gold, a solid gold lion and a solid gold vat jar. The whole lot weighed 8,500kg.

In 90 BC Roman legionnaire soldiers were paid 12 pieces of gold a year (worth about £2000).

SOLID GOLD FACT

The most anyone has ever paid for one gold coin was £4.7 million.

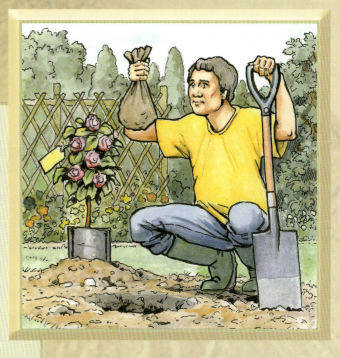

If you are very lucky you might find a coin hoard. Before there were banks, people would bury their money in the ground. If you find a bag of coins, it is because the owner didn't get round to digging it up. Why do you think someone might not dig up his or her coins?

More gold is bought and sold in India than any other country. Here, people keep their money as gold jewellery.

Gold is kept as bars by some banks.

Gold is rare

Only about 125,000 tonnes of gold has ever been mined. Most of it is still being used today. If you put it all together you could fit it inside a small house.

Gold is found in sea water. In a 1 kilometre cube of sea water there are 6 kilograms of pure gold. It would be too expensive to get the gold out of the water.

Today, gold is mined. It is dug out of rock. Sometimes the gold has mixed with other things, and the miners have to 'clean' it to make pure gold.

They 'clean' the gold by melting it, or washing it with strong, poisonous chemicals.

Finding gold

Gold is found all over the world, but some places have more of it than others.

Mali

There is a lot of gold in Mali. Mansa Musa was a king of Mali. He was a Muslim and in 1324 he set out to go to Mecca. He took with him 80 camels, each carrying 136 kg of gold.

At that time in Africa, you could trade the same weight of gold for salt, which was also precious.

Ghana

Ghana has a lot of gold. Gold has been mined in Ghana for over 2000 years. Ghana used to be called the 'Gold Coast'.

The Ashanti (say 'Ash – an – ti') people in Ghana became very rich from mining gold.

There is a story about how the Ashanti people became strong.

In the late 17th Century...

A priest called together all the arguing chiefs.

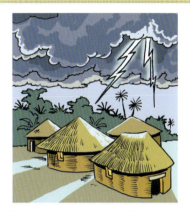

There was a thunderstorm.

The priest called to the gods and a golden stool fell from the sky.

It landed beside one chief,

who became the ruler.

From then on all the Ashanti people worked together and became very powerful.

In the 17th Century the Dutch, Portugese and British captured Ghanaians to sell as slaves. They made more money selling slaves than they did selling gold. Gold miners were caught and sent to work as slaves. The skills of the miners were nearly forgotten. The Ashanti people are no longer rich but there is still some gold mining today.

USA

In 1848 a gold nugget was found in California. It had been washed out of the hills by a river.

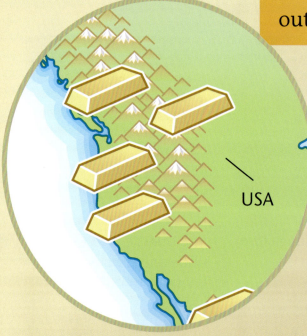

Gold Nuggets

By 1852 nearly 275,000 gold seekers had rushed to California. This was called the Gold Rush. To start with, miners could get gold from the rivers. But this 'easy' gold was soon all collected. Then gold mining machines were invented.

There were other 'Gold Rushes' to other countries. In the 19th Century over 10,000 Chinese miners went to Australia to help mine for new gold found there.

South Africa

South Africa is now the world's largest gold producer.

Most of the gold is underground and some modern mines go down 3.8 km.

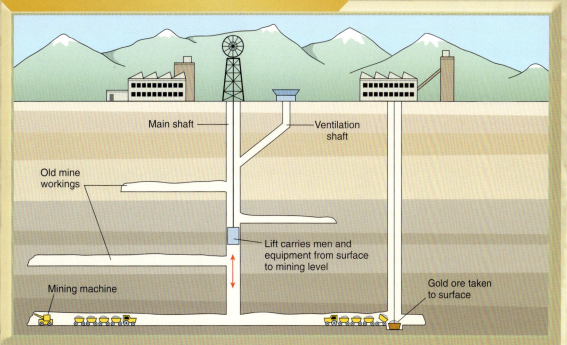

Gold is weighed in troy ounces. 1 troy ounce = 31g
To make 1 troy ounce of gold it takes:
- 38 hours of work.
- 6400 litres of water.
- enough electricity to run a big house for 10 days.
- over 11 cubic metres of compressed air.
- poison.

Panning for gold

If you're lucky, you can find gold in river beds. It has been washed out of rocks by the river. This is called panning for gold.

You will need a shallow pan.

Put it in the river.

Take it out and swill it about. Let the water spill over the edge.

Look at anything you catch in your pan. Wash it with clean water. You may find grains or even nuggets of gold.

Have you heard of the story of the Golden Fleece? Well, the Greeks used to pan for gold, but instead of using a pan, they used sheepskins. The woolly hair was good for catching little grains of gold.

Five facts about gold

1: You get a gold record for selling 500,000 copies.

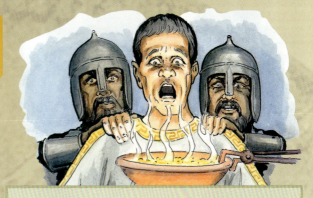

2: Crassus was a greedy Roman statesman. He was killed by having molten gold poured down his throat.

3: Gold is used in medicines for bone illnesses and eye and ear diseases.

4: If all the gold ever found was made into the thinnest possible gold wire (thinner than a human hair), it would go round the world about 72 million times.

5: Gold has always been recycled because it is expensive. It is melted down and used again for something else. This stud might be made of gold that was once in a Pharaoh's mouth!

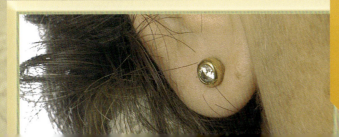

The Midas Touch

There is a legend that a god granted King Midas a wish when he was kind to an old man.

About 710 BC

Midas wished that everything he touched would turn into gold.

So everything Midas touched turned into gold.

When he sat down to eat, all his food turned to gold.

Then he touched his daughter and she turned to gold.

Midas realised his wish had been a stupid one. He pleaded with the god to help him.

He was told to wash his hands in a sacred river. Everything turned back to what it was.

In ancient times, you could find gold nuggets in this sacred river.

Look back

1 What did the Incas call gold?

2 What can hallmarks tell us about a gold object?

3 Why is there a film of gold on firefighters' suits?

4 What is the most important use for gold today?

5 Name two countries which have gold mines.

Index

Anglo-Saxon	2
carat	7
Egyptian	4, 8
electricity	3, 10
firefighters	11
Ghana	16, 17
gold	
bar	13
leaf	6
record	21
rush	18
wire	9
hallmark	7
heat	3, 11
Inca	5
jewellery	4, 5, 9
machines	10
Mali	15
mine/mining	14, 16, 18, 19, 20
money	12
pulled	3, 9
rare	3, 14
Romans	9, 12
rust	8
sea water	14
shiny	3, 4
soft	3, 6
South Africa	20
space shuttle	11
Sun	4, 5
teeth	8
USA	18
use (of gold)	5, 8, 10

23

Glossary

Anglo-Saxon: The form of Old English spoken before 1066.

carat: A measure of the amount of pure gold in an object. The higher the carat the purer the gold.

conduct: To conduct electricity or heat is to allow it to pass along.

gold leaf: Very thin sheets of gold.

hallmark: Symbols hammered into something gold which tells you how pure the gold is, when the object was made, and sometimes where it was made.

Mecca: The holiest place in the Islamic religion. All Muslims must go to Mecca at least once in their lives.

mine: A place where coal, jewels or precious metals are dug out of the ground.

nugget: A rough lump of gold.